Karreecha, Write!

"What I discovered on a 30-day Sabbatical"

Karreecha Newby

1

Copyright @2024

Cover Design by: Karreecha Newby

Edited by: Karreecha Newby

"I will instruct thee and teach thee in the way which thou shalt go: I will guide thee with mine eye." Psalm 32:8 KJV

TABLE OF CONTENTS

Setting the Stage

About Me

I am deeply committed to personal growth, healing, and purpose. I am introspective, constantly seeking divine guidance, and am attuned to the inner workings of my emotions and spirituality. My reflections on past experiences-both positive and negative, like trauma, helps me to align myself with God's will and remain open to growth, even when it's challenging.

I am a compassionate leader and mental health advocate-helping others navigate their emotional and spiritual journeys. I am thoughtful and sometimes analytical, so I offer my administrative gift by showing incredible attention to detail, which can be seen throughout my career, ranging from my work in early intervention to studying emotions like anger, anxiety, and depression. At the same time, I prioritize alignment with the right people, fostering relationships that uplift and sharpen one another—demonstrating a clear value for meaningful, purposeful connections.

I work diligently to approach life with both humility and strength, embracing divine correction and celebrating moments of clarity and inspiration. I embrace my dreams, desires, and passions while honoring my ongoing healing process. I am one who is deeply rooted in faith and resilience while cultivating an ongoing relationship with Jesus Christ.

Introduction to the concept of a sabbatical

At the end of April and onset of May 2024, I felt a profound calling to "come away" – to retreat from the noise and be with The Father. Merriam Webster's Dictionary defines a sabbatical as a break or change from a normal routine (as of employment). Additionally, "sabbatical" is an adjective referring to the observance of the Sabbath, as in "sabbatical laws." The Bible clearly states that a sabbatical is a time for rest. From the beginning of time, as written in Genesis 2:3, "God blessed the seventh day and made it holy, because on it, He rested from all the work of creating what he had done." If rest was important to God, it should be equally important to us as believers.

At the onset of creation, God rested on the seventh day after completing His work (Genesis 2:2-3). While this was not an act of Him being 'fatigued or tired', this was a deliberate action to set a pattern for all of humanity. The sanctification of the seventh day underscores its importance.

Recently, I had a long conversation with my uncle who recently passed away. About a year ago, I literally fussed at him, consistently telling him that He owed God many *sabbaths* and that is why He was being made to lie down. On a serious note, he had fallen ill and was forced to stay on bedrest. But what is it about rest that God has ordained it for us. Let's look at what is written in Exodus 20:8-11 and how we are to uphold The Fourth Commandment emphasizing this principle: "Remember the Sabbath day, to keep it holy". Perhaps, God wants us to "stop doing all the stuff" and "get still, relax, learn to trust and depend on Him". There is so much peace in letting go of all the "stuff" to become utterly unhinged and unattached to the "things of this world". Now, that's not to say that I don't have times where I get busy and sort of become the master, but when I realize that I am relying on self to get things done, I get back into alignment or cultivate a place of rest.

Are you seriously depending on God? Can He be trusted while you are awake as well as while you are asleep? Does He have a good track record of working on your behalf? Can you be led by still waters so while He restores your soul from whatever you have experienced during the week or from whatever has affected you? When do you find time for rest?

Jesus reinforced the importance of rest in His teachings and practices. He stated in Mark 2:27 that "The *Sabbath* was made for man, not man for the *Sabbath*". He encouraged rest and He sought solitude. Rest is a gift from God.

Like Jesus, after intense periods of teaching, healing and ministering in whatever capacity, we need to learn to prioritize our own time of rest. In 2023, I talked to so many people about the need for rest and explained that I am regimented when it came to my schedule-to include rest. For me, it was another level of learning to trust God. Especially someone who is always taking the lead on things, events, projects, and the like. I must often go away and "take my fill of rest". Friends laughed because, if they called or texted me at a certain time of day, I would tell them that I was resting. They assumed that I was asleep or taking a nap, but no, I was 'resting my heart'. Most of the time, I was on a hydromassage table at the gym, trying to regulate my body after extended time of driving or being in classrooms.

The Difference Between Rest and Sleep

In short, the difference between Rest and Sleep is that "rest" involves taking a step back to reset, being mindful of surroundings, and releasing control over external factors or things that you have no control over. Rest can include activities like relaxing, meditating, or simply pausing from active engagements to rejuvenate. While "sleep" is when the body tunes out external and environmental factors, becoming unaware of its surroundings. During sleep, the body and mind go through various cycles to restore and repair themselves on a deeper level. Rest is more of a conscious and active state of relaxation, while sleep is an unconscious state, essentially while your body and mind recover.

It's amazing how something as simple as rest can have such a profound impact on our emotional responses and ability to handle stress. One of the things that I discovered about myself is that when I am well rested, I tend to have a greater capacity to take on more tasks. When I am well regulated, my responses to stressful events or tasks are less reactive. One of the things I also recommend to others, when they appear overly anxious or dysregulated, is a "nap" of some sort. Yes, I know, "naps are for the kiddos", but beloved, you are God's kiddo, so incorporate naps in your day somehow.

Practical Implications for Modern Believers

Incorporating rest into daily life can be challenging in our fast-paced world. However, it is essential for maintaining a healthy balance between work and personal well-being. We all can start by setting aside specific times for rest and reflection, ensuring that we honor the principle of the *Sabbath*. Balancing work and rest involve recognizing that we are limited in what we can do in our own strength and capabilities while trusting in God's provision. It requires intentionality and discipline to create space for rest amidst our responsibilities.

The Lead-up to the Sabbatical

In the months leading up to the decision to rest and retreat, I found myself traversing the United States, moving back and forth across different time zones on a weekly basis. From February 2024 onwards, my life was a whirlwind of flights, airports and hotels, with little time to pause and reflect. The constant travel began to take a toll on me, both physically and mentally. While I appreciate, celebrate, and embrace every opportunity I have been afforded, the jetlag and exhaustion were undeniable. On top of that, I had recently moved back to my childhood hometown and was actively working through such a big transition. It took a lot of physical and emotional energy as well. To say the least, I had multiple transitions happening at once.

Deciding to Retreat

By May, the fatigue of continuous travel had set in. I wasn't just tired; I was a bit weary. In this state, the call to retreat and reconnect with The Father came at a critical juncture. This 30-day *sabbatical* was not only timely but also essential. I needed to reassess and realign, to ensure that I was on His timeline, doing the right things, with the right people and executing His purpose effectively. Many might argue that Old Testament scriptures about rest no longer apply, but I believe otherwise. Understanding and implementing biblical principles (as much as possible) is a daily practice for me. For instance, God instructed Joshua to "meditate on the Law Day and night" in Joshua 1:8. You cannot just enter meditation haphazardly, it is intentional and takes time to quiet down the mind. However, by examining how God dealt with people in the past, helps me to properly steward my life in terms of rest. So, if I am going to strive for anything, I strive to apply "the need to rest".

Practices During the Sabbatical

Before embarking on my spiritual retreat, I delved into research to combat the fatigue I was experiencing. I discovered that a combination of adequate rest, hydration, and a consistent exercise regimen could significantly alleviate exhaustion. I committed to making the most of this *sabbatical* while incorporating these practices into my daily routine. During this time, I prioritized my activities-ensuring that I got ample sleep to recover from the months of travel. I also increased my water intake, understanding the crucial role hydration plays in maintaining physical and mental well-being.

I also "asked for help" because I needed it. For example, I asked for help with meal prep, as extensive travel can sometimes cause one to have a poor diet and I needed to take my discipline to another level-in order to keep my mind active and sharp. This period of retreat was more than just a physical recharge. It was a time of deep spiritual renewal. Some of the time was spent in prayer and meditation and some days I fasted while seeking The Lord's guidance and clarity about my present, my next, and my future. The quiet moments allowed me to reflect on my journey, the lessons learned, and the path ahead.

The Whisper: "May is Mayhem"

It's profound how the Holy Spirit communicates, especially during moments when we might not be fully alert, due to extreme fatigue or some other physical experience; He knows how to get our attention. You might ask, "how has this helped me to understand the necessity of discernment and how I would approach subtle nudges in the future". Well, this experience has deeply impacted my approach to discernment. It taught me the importance of being spiritually and physically alert, especially during moments of fatigue or after significant tasks. I've learned to pay closer attention to those subtle whispers and take time to process what the Father is trying to communicate. Now, when I sense similar warnings, I make an intentional effort to pause, reflect, lean-in and seek clarity rather than dismissing them due to tiredness. This experience underscored the importance of diligently balancing rest with spiritual vigilance. We can all improve in staying alert and truly paying attention. Additionally, seeking the prayers of others is also vital to successfully fulfilling our purpose.

During the early morning hours in April, I would hear a whisper, "Mayhem." When I heard this, I leaned in to see what else the Father would say. Now, you may sort of know what mayhem means, but others may not. For the sake of understanding, Merriam Webster's Dictionary defines mayhem as "actions that hurt people and destroy things; a scene or situation that involves a lot of violence." I'll never forget, April 17th, 2024, to be exact – I was leaving Ft. Myers, Florida, where I was on assignment for work. It was the last part of the assignment, and I was preparing to leave. As I packed my clothes and headed to the car, the Holy Spirit began to speak expressly to me about "attacks that were coming." I think because I was so tired, I heard Him, but I didn't necessarily process, conceptualize or internalize it.

Spiritual Warfare and Revelation

In the month of May, I mean, right at the door, I experienced what seemed to be a series of strategized or manufactured attacks in almost every area of my life, financially, physically, mentally, and emotionally. It was a huge undertaking, but I knew that I needed the help of The Holy Spirit. The first thing I noticed is that at some point, I seemed to offend people for the smallest things. Things that I could typically have conversations about or say to certain people, appeared to come off as "offensive" or it was taken personally. Or, perhaps, I just did not frame my words the right way. So, I did a lot of apologizing and "letting people be people" (because we know people be out here in the world peopling anyways). Several members of my family were hospitalized due to unforeseen health related incidents. My email account was hacked, and hackers had gained access to my banking information. They were almost successful in gaining access to my money, and this event was one of the most stressful situations that I had ever encountered.

I was unable to access funds through any electronic means in any way possible. I started doing business "the old school way by going inside the bank". I did not do any online banking during the month of May, nor did I even look at my accounts electronically. I was already dealing with fatigue and exhaustion; I was stretched emotionally and mentally (psychological). Due to so many demanding activities that were identified as 'attacks from the enemy', projects such as launching my book were delayed. I had to drive back and forth out of town to do banking as my bank was not in the city where I resided. It seemed like I was in a whirlwind.

Reflecting on the onset of the onslaught, I heard the Holy Spirit remind me that the attacks are "indications of what was coming" and I needed to remain focused. I kept reminding myself that "spiritual warfare can sometimes be a precursor to blessings", but I needed to steward well. Rest was the remedy during this time. Most everything that occurred was out of my control, so I had to use what I had within my realm of access: praise, worship, prayer, and rest.

Revelatory Dreams

Before all the disruption broke out, I experienced various dreams back in March and April (2024), each with distinct themes. One dream stood out for its profound implication on relationships, alignments, and fellowship. The revelations deeply influenced my understanding of my interactions and connections with others. In the dream, I stood with two respected individuals whose identities I will keep confidential. I extended my right hand several times to one of them, hoping to establish fellowship. Each time the person withdrew their hand, revealing a painful boil or severe blister on their palm, I heard, "If I show her my hand, she will know my hands are unclean." Though I understood the situation, I continued to extend my hand, demonstrating that my only intent was to offer fellowship without judgment.

I also had another dream where I found myself back at my grandmother's house—a symbol of delay and foundational issues. Someone had taken all my personal information and scattered it across the ground. Papers containing details about my life, bank account information, and private conversations lay exposed in one place. I managed to gather everything into a large black trash bag. However, in the dream, I distinctly thought to myself, "Whoever did this knows me well; they are very familiar with me"—a sign of a familiar spirit (I'll share more about this at another time). From this, we can conclude that perhaps the email situation could have been a lot worse or aborted altogether if I had not received the warning dream.

Interpretation and Realization of dreams

As I share this next section with you, Psalm 24:4 comes to mind, where David describes the requirements for standing in God's presence: "The one who has clean hands and a pure heart, who does not trust in an idol or swear by a false god."

This verse emphasizes the qualities needed to enter God's presence—purity, integrity, and genuine devotion. During this time, I was praying for future contacts and for those I was already in fellowship with. Initially, I reflected on my dreams, seeking insights from others. Only a week later did I realize the dream wasn't solely about the other person—it also had significance for me. It highlighted my tendency to extend myself to people who were not good for me or meant to be in fellowship with me or vice versa. I needed to increase my understanding of discernment, and my discernment needed to go to another level. This realization also shed light on an unhealthy pattern of relating that I've had since childhood, stemming from relational trauma or "abandonment". There was another revelation that came out of this dream, but I will reserve to share later.

Let me be clearer, it does not mean that people are bad, but it simply means that God is good, and He knows what we should be doing in terms of purpose. This *sabbatical* has been insightful and has helped me to reflect on the importance of discernment in relationships. Recognizing that God has a blueprint for our lives is essential, as it reassures us that He knows the connections and relationships that will aid us on our journey. Just like a trip to the grocery store fulfills a specific purpose, some relationships are designed to serve a particular need or complete an assignment in a specific season. Once that purpose is fulfilled, it's time to move on, just as we leave the store once we've completed our shopping. We do not have to disconnect from people, but we need to ensure that our focus is on what "we are suppose" to be doing" with "those we are suppose to be doing it with" or we stand to frustrate our God ordained assignment.

However, it requires spiritual maturity and the guidance of the Holy Spirit to distinguish between transactional relationships and those meant for cultivation. Not all connections are meant to be long-term, but each has a role in fulfilling God's plan for our lives. This perspective encourages me to seek God's wisdom regarding relationships, ensuring that we remain aligned with His purpose rather than becoming attached to connections that may no longer serve our spiritual journey.

Let this serve as a reminder of the importance of obedience and attentiveness to the Holy Spirit, trusting that He will guide us to the right people and opportunities that align with God's perfect plan.

One other dream that I had during this time was a dream where my braces were coming off my teeth and it caused my teeth to move. I had that dream several times. We know that braces are for 'correction' and 'alignment' so I sort of knew what The Father was saying to me about 'correction'. It is so imperative that when The Father speaks to us in a dream that we search Him out to know exactly what He is saying and how we need to respond.

We know that God loves us enough to communicate with us in our dreams, reveal His plan, and to give us instructions. All of what had taken place in May was an attempt to delay purpose. Additionally, being in alignment with the wrong people can also delay the plans of God as well, but I am grateful for the correction and alignment He was bringing to keep me on track.

I am very grateful that The Father offers both guidance and a course for correction when needed. The symbolism of braces—meant to correct and align—resonates deeply with how God works in our lives, ensuring that we stay on the right path, even when things attempt to delay purpose.

Personal Reflection and Growth

I have made significant strides in my healing journey, but I recognize that I am still a work in progress. I've always had a "savior complex," believing I could make others better or help them. However, this dream was a divine message urging me to "understand the assignment" during this season. My task is to comprehend what is mandated or required, which will in turn, help me understand who I am supposed to connect with. We must stay attuned to God's voice, and to remain vigilant in aligning ourselves with the right people and circumstances to stay on track with His purpose.

The dreams also helped me understand more how God feels about us having healthy relationships. As I continue to heal and grow, I aim to connect with individuals who I am meant to be in fellowship with, who will not only challenge me, but embrace what God is doing in and through me, and I am to do the same for them. The "iron sharpens iron" scripture beautifully captures the essence of mutually beneficial relationships, where both parties are strengthened and refined through their connection (Proverbs 27:17, KJV).

Finally, anything outside of doing relationships or anything the way God intends it, brings about delay and can sometimes kill the assignment altogether. That, my friend, is just too unkind. So, what I believe the Lord is saying to all of us is, "trim the fat" or to cut out everything that is not connected to purpose, so we can realize potential for ourselves and the world around us.

Restoration, Rejuvenation, & Recalibration

Importance of rest for the body and mind

During my 30-day *sabbatical*, I continued working but eliminated extracurricular activities to focus solely on essential tasks (like launching my book). One significant change that I implemented was drastically reducing screen time, including social media. I disconnected without any announcements, while stopping the extended time of scrolling. Additionally, I minimized my interactions with people, sharing my experience with only a select few who discerned the need to pray for me. This period of isolation raised concerns among some who reached out, fearing something was wrong. However, this time allowed me to concentrate intensely on the messages from The Holy Spirit, free from distractions (the beauty of being single).

By removing myself from social media and other digital distractions, I found that my mind was clearer, my emotions were more stable, and my heart was at peace. My members (heart and mind) agreed with one another-synchronizing and harmonizing. The constant barrage of information and the compulsion to stay connected can overwhelm the brain, leading to stress and anxiety. Without these distractions, I focused better.

Also, during this time, I also kept my conversations to a minimum. This was not out of a desire for isolation, but rather to avoid unnecessary interference. The quiet allowed me to listen more intently to The Holy Spirit's guidance. Without the usual noise and interruptions, I could achieve a level of focus that was otherwise unattainable. This period of solitude was not loneliness but a deliberate step to nurture my spiritual and mental health.

Clinical Perspective on Sleep as Rest

From a clinical standpoint, extended periods of "broken rest" can lead to numerous issues, including emotional dysregulation and cognitive fog. When the body does not receive adequate, uninterrupted rest, it struggles to function optimally. Sleep is essential for repairing and resetting the body and its functions, such as regulating emotions as I shared earlier. However, lack of rest can impair judgment, reduce productivity, and increase the risk of mental health disorders.

My 30-day *sabbatical* underscored the importance of rest for both my body and mind. This experience highlighted that sometimes, taking a step back and disconnecting is necessary to recharge and maintain well-being. In our fast-paced world, prioritizing our activities is not just beneficial but essential for a healthy, balanced life.

Spiritual insights and highlights

During my 30-day *sabbatical*, I experienced a series of spiritual insights and memory recalls that provided a deeper understanding of my life's journey. These flashbacks, particularly from my early childhood, revealed significant moments that have shaped who I am today. The Holy Spirit highlighted these memories, showing me the importance of my early experiences and how they continue to influence my present path. So many times, we miss the "Clarion Call" that another season is upon us or that we need to shift trajectories. Had I not pulled away, just for a season, I would have missed what the Lord was trying to get me to see.

Early Childhood Memories

Early childhood memories are often deeply significant, especially when the Holy Spirit brings them to the forefront. Memories can serve as keys to understanding aspects of our identity, behavior patterns, and even unresolved emotional or spiritual issues. The Holy Spirit's role in highlighting these memories is often to bring healing, insight, and clarity to areas of our lives that may have been impacted by early experiences.

According to John 14:26, KJV, it is the Holy Spirit's job to bring things back to our remembrance, those things that The Father has said to us. Sometimes, the Father even reveals things to us at an early age. When the Holy Spirit brings up early childhood memories, it's important to approach them with openness and a willingness to seek God's perspective on those moments. These memories can reveal patterns or strongholds that need to be broken, areas where forgiveness is needed, or places where God wants to bring restoration and wholeness. So, I would find myself thinking, "why are you showing me this" or "why am I seeing that"?

The significance lies in the fact that God desires us to be whole and free, and sometimes that journey requires revisiting our past with His guidance. By doing so, we can better understand how those early experiences have shaped us and allow God to realign our thinking, heal any wounds, and restore what was lost or damaged. This process of revisiting and healing early memories is a powerful way that God prepares us to step into our divine purpose with greater clarity and freedom.

For example, at the cusp of May, I began having vivid flashbacks or memories of my childhood. One prominent memory that The Holy

Spirit kept highlighting was the reality of my learning to read at a very young age. He specifically highlighted a time that I was about six or seven years old, and I helped my older cousin with his homework. I vividly remember standing around my grandmother's table, confidently saying, "Grandma, I can do it." I think what God does is so awesome and how He plants gifts and talents in us that cannot necessarily been seen with the naked eye. The fact that I was drawn to activities like teaching, writing, and even the structure of language speaks to the gifts that were being nurtured within me, even before I fully understood their significance.

Question to ponder:

What are your natural and innate abilities and how is what you're doing now connected?

Another memory that was highlighted was those times I would sit at the kitchen table in our childhood home, pretending to type. I am not sure where I got the notion to type as I was not around anyone who did any administrative work. I am sure I saw it somewhere in my mind but was never introduced to typing until the ninth grade. But I would sit at the kitchen table as a little girl and peck as though I was typing. This table was also where my sisters and I played school, with me always assuming the role of the teacher. These activities were not just games; they were early expressions of my imagination and passion for learning, teaching, reading and writing.

Spiritual Revelations

The Holy Spirit highlighted these memories, revealing their deeper spiritual significance and why rest is so very important because it helps us to make sense of what God is speaking to us. The clear vision of helping my cousin and the consistent role of playing the teacher were more than just childhood activities; they were indicators of my early calling, gifting, and talents that spoke to my God Ordained Destiny.

Another significant revelation was the 'open visions' I had as a child, where I saw myself sitting in front of a great white throne taking notes (this continued even until I became an adult). These visions stood out so much during the month of May that I began to pray and meditate on their meanings. I knew that they were divine messages, pointing towards my innate abilities and the path I was meant to follow.

A verse that resonated deeply with these experiences is Psalm 32:8: "I will instruct thee and teach thee in the way which thou shalt go: I will guide thee with mine eye." This scripture encapsulates the guidance and direction I felt during my *sabbatical*, reaffirming that my journey is divinely led because He is acquainted with all my ways. And for this season, I am to "focus and develop my craft for writing".

Realization

To confirm these memories, I called my mother and asked if she remembered my learning to read and write. She not only confirmed but also recounted how I used to "play school" and teach my sisters everything I learned. These conversations validated my memories and underscored their importance. Naturally, as I grew into adulthood, I took on roles that supported my childhood dreams and imagination.

Again, I learned to type in the ninth grade. However, I now type over 70 words per minute, mostly error-free. Journaling became a significant part of my life while navigating challenging seasons.

Journaling served as an outlet for me to express my thoughts and emotions. I have so many journals filled with sermon notes, poems, thoughts, songs, and drawings. These early habits fostered my love for writing and personal and professional growth. Can you see the Lord's leading in what I am sharing? I am sure that you can resonate with this, as at some point, hopefully, you too will start to take inventory of your life if you have not already.

Professional Development

My early experiences naturally led to a career in secretarial studies and legal work. I obtained a degree (AS & BS) in Secretarial Studies and became a legal secretary for a probate attorney in my early twenties. My skills in probate law were exceptional, and I started with the attorney as a Paralegal, right after graduating with an Associate's degree in Office Administration (Legal Studies). His legal secretary, a classmate of mine, recruited me on the day of graduation, recognizing my excellence in probate law. I literally left graduation and started my job the same day. While I excelled in probate law, my true passion lies in helping people and being with those I assisted. This nurtured my self-esteem and provided a sense of fulfillment.

The spiritual insights and vivid memories I experienced during my *sabbatical* have provided profound clarity for RIGHT NOW-God's prophetic timeline for my life. This period of reflection has underscored the importance of understanding and embracing one's past to navigate the present and future with purpose and clarity. The guidance of Psalm 32:8 has been a comforting reminder that I am being led on the right path, both spiritually and professionally.

Understanding Your Assignment for The Season

Clarifying Priorities of the Father

What is the significance of clarity? Why do we need to be clear on what God asks of us? How often do you ask Him about His priorities and what's on His heart for you?

Clarity is vital in our spiritual, emotional, and practical lives. It represents a clear understanding, a vision of where we are headed, and insight into God's will for us. When we achieve clarity, we can see past distractions, confusion, and uncertainty, allowing us to make decisions aligned with our purpose and God's direction. Spiritually, clarity enables us to discern God's voice more distinctly, recognizing His guidance amid the noise of everyday life. It helps us avoid being swayed by the wrong influences and remain steadfast in our faith and mission. With clarity, we can better understand God's instructions, which leads to a more focused and intentional life.

Emotionally, clarity brings peace and a sense of settlement. It reduces anxiety and stress that come from indecision, apprehension or uncertainty. Knowing the path, we should take and why we're taking it allows us to move forward with confidence and assurance. It also helps us identify and release anything that doesn't align with God's purpose for us, including unhealthy relationships, habits, or thoughts. A lot of times, when I am invited to participate on a project and I sense a level of unsettledness or angst with it, I will sometimes retreat and ask the person to spell out what it is that they are trying to accomplish. If they are not sure, then a lot of times, I proceed with caution or I ask for some sort of "raincheck".

Practically, clarity allows us to set achievable goals and make actionable plans. It guides our steps and ensures that our efforts are not wasted on pursuits that do not lead us toward our calling. It helps us prioritize what truly matters, reducing overwhelm and helping us stay on track. In all, clarity is a gift that brings purpose, peace, and progress. It's an essential aspect of living a life that honors God and fulfills the unique calling He has placed on each of us.

One of the things that consistently work on is "understanding God's priority for the season". Anyone who knows me knows that I like to assign my day-meaning, I like to account for what I am doing throughout the days. Although spontaneous at times, I can get a little analytical about my time and efforts. One day, I was corrected by the Holy Spirit after ending a call with a friend who I had planned to do all this amazing stuff with for the upcoming year. As soon as I ended the phone call, The Holy Spirit dropped this scripture in my mind, "Commit thy way unto the Lord; trust also in him; and he shall bring it to pass" (Psalm 37:5, KJV). I called my friend and asked her if we could "table" the plans we made. She was very understanding as I explained to her what The Holy Spirit had revealed.

One early morning in May (2024), I began to get promptings to "Pray over my destiny". As I stated earlier, during the month of May, my dreams increased as some seemed to be instructions and others were clearly warning dreams. I had a very disturbing dream that when I awoke, I went right into prayer. The Holy spirit was leading me to pray for myself extensively as well as the destinies of children. I didn't quite understand, but I just prayed as I was led, as I had been instructed to pray for children on many occasions.

One of the things the Holy Spirit began to reveal to me was how important it is that if we, as adults, (whether you have children or not) are to expand the Kingdom of God, that we must be in the right place at the right time doing the right things with the right people. When we begin to discern the season and the assignment, as previously shared, we find ourselves connecting with the right people. The assignments and instructions come from God whether they be to develop a business idea, close a business, or something else. His Kingdom expands when people are not only activated in their giftings or callings but operating in their gifting serving purpose, whether it be in the workplace, church ministry or another branch of ministry of some sort. We need to find ourselves one hundred percent submitted to the 'call' of the season. Like me, if you are someone who has gone through extended warfare, in my opinion, it appears that the fights have been over "revelation and clarity about our assignment".

Dear Parents, "Children are God's Heritage"

As we navigate the journey of raising children, it's essential and urgent to remember that "Children are God's Heritage." This highlights our role as adult caregivers and parents in nurturing the legacy and future generations that God has entrusted to us. To fulfill this divine responsibility, we must align ourselves with what is important to Him. From the moment a child is born, their purpose is set in motion, and it is our duty to ensure they receive the emotional, physical, and spiritual nourishment (equipping) they need. With that being said, "pay attention to what children are naturally good at and the types of things they take interest" in.

Understanding that children are of utmost importance to God compels us to create environments conducive to their growth and spiritual development. Throughout my recent *sabbatical*, the Holy Spirit continuously reminded me of the significance of early guidance and direction. These reminders stemmed from personal experiences and biblical revelations, particularly highlighting the importance of childhood in shaping one's destiny. While I did not necessarily have anyone guiding me, I am so grateful that "The Father's Hand has always been on my life" as revealed by The Holy Spirit (and confirmed by a minister I hold in high regard).

It is the reason why some attacks of the enemy did not work. I also wrote about this in another book that I published entitled, "The Call: Conversations and Encounters". As parents, it is imperative to be actively involved in your child's life, steering them towards their God-given purpose. My own journey is a testament to the impact of early influences and guidance. Although my mother wasn't a practicing Christian, she ensured I attended church sometimes with my cousin. I believe the little exposure that I had in a faith-filled (church) environment played a crucial role in my spiritual development.

Psalm 127:3-5 - A Divine Reminder

The Holy Spirit repeatedly brought to my attention Psalm 127:3-5: *"Children are indeed a heritage from the LORD, and the fruit of the womb is His reward. Like arrows in the hand of a warrior, so are children born in one's youth. Blessed is the man whose quiver is full of them. He will not be put to shame when he confronts the enemies at the gate."*

This scripture emphasizes that children are a reward from God, likened to arrows in a warrior's hand. It signifies the importance of directing our children with precision and purpose. A warrior carefully aims arrows to hit their target, just as we must guide our children towards their divine destinies. This means that a lot of their life must be governed, guarded, and they must be guided. We do not need to control them or get into power struggles, but they do need to be protected. We can be friendly and have fun with our children, but we are not their friends. We do not reduce ourselves to "sis or bruh" when it comes to our children.

Being Present and Hands-On

In this season, God is calling us to be present and hands-on in our children's lives. To witness the manifestations of the Kingdom in their lives, we must actively participate in their upbringing. As we embrace our role as stewards of God's heritage, let us commit to nurturing our children emotionally, physically, and spiritually. By doing so, we ensure they are positioned to fulfill their God-given purposes as we are. Remember, each child is a precious arrow in the quiver of God's warrior, destined to hit their target with precision and impact. Let us, therefore, be diligent in our responsibility, guiding our children towards their divine destinies with love, faith, and unwavering commitment. Again, *"Pray, Pray, pray"* over the destiny of your children and those they are in company with.

A Divine Directive to Write

I have shared with you how I experienced profound moments of clarity and divine inspiration during my *sabbatical*. These revelations were pivotal in understanding my life's purpose and the direction I needed to take for this moment of time (prophetic timeline). The Holy Spirit provided clear guidance, emphasizing the importance of my present assignment and the steps necessary to fulfill it.

One of the most significant moments occurred on my way home from North Carolina in May (2024). As I was dozing off on the plane, I distinctly heard in my right ear, "Karreecha, Write! Write,

Karreecha!" The message was so clear and resounding that it immediately woke me up. This moment was the genesis of the title for this book and the clarity I needed for my assignment this season. The directive to write was unmistakable, and I promptly designated specific days to focus on writing. I pulled out my phone and I plugged in the days that I would solely focus on strengthening my craft.

I usually return home on a Saturday evening and would have to 'will' myself out of bed on Sundays to make it to church due to the 'jet lag'. On a particular Sunday in May (2024), I decided to visit with a friend, and it was there that the Lord confirmed exactly what He had been saying to me all month long. The pastor who is a local Apostle was closing out the morning sermon-while walking up and down the aisle praying for people. Once at my row, this person looked at me and said, "write, write, write and REST in that" and casually walked off.

It sealed it for me because earlier in the year, I started to feel a little angst and I started to ask the lord, what's a priority for now because I wanted to ensure that I was doing the right thing, at the right time, with the right people for the right people, using the right resources. I often ask myself and others, "how much of what you are doing comes from the Lord".

Are we just existing day to day expecting outcomes, or are we spending time asking God, "what's a priority for Him". I do not like wasting time and I do not like wasting the time of others. Here is what I can tell you about this 30-day *sabbatical*, "it was time well spent". I came away with fresh ideas and insight on how I would accomplish what He has ordained for this season.

The funny thing is that what I am bringing to you through this writing is REST! Whatever He is speaking to you, REST in that! It is easier when you have His approval and His assurance to do what He has ordained you to do.

Connecting the Dots

I remember having a dream recently about connecting dots. In the dream, a certain person was assuring me that "it would all come together". I literally awoke from the dream writing and drawing what I saw. The Father began to connect the dots for me, revealing that I was born to write and record His words. As I have begun to embrace this calling, I started researching courses, books, videos, and workshops related to writing and the scribal anointing. To my surprise and delight, I discovered an institution that helps individuals like me understand "The role of the Scribe and the scribal anointing." This revelation was a confirmation that God had been preparing me for "such a time as this" all my life. And NOW is the season for it!

Training and Preparation

Most of my training has come through personal prayer time, where I have learned to listen to the voice of The Father and instructions, and through my job experiences. I have received extensive training in communication and writing, and in nearly every job I have held, I have taken on the role of a secretary or administrator of some sort. This pattern continued in my church ministry, where I also served in secretarial roles (almost every time) as well as business meetings. These experiences have been part of God's preparation for me to step into my ordained purpose as a 'Recorder' or 'Scribe'.

The Importance of Being in Place

It is crucial that everyone is in their respective places, doing what they are ordained to do. It's no longer enough to just be gifted; God wants to perfect and sanctify the gifts He has given us-while "trimming the fat" or letting go of the mundane tasks that sometimes is not connected to purpose. Some things may be good things, but they are not 'God Ordained' things. The Father desires us to become experts in our calling, moving beyond surface-level ministry to a deeper, more committed level where we can have lasting impact on people and the world at large. Many are praying for revival, a move and more of God, but He is saying, "If you want more, give me more to work with." This call to discipline and total compliance or surrender requires us to wholly dedicate ourselves to what He has called us to do. This is about destiny, and it is going to take a regimented and regulated mindset to fulfill and accomplish "The Great Commission" to Go!

The moments of clarity and divine inspiration I experienced during my *sabbatical* have profoundly impacted my understanding of my purpose. Here is what I want you to take away:

- **Clarifying Priorities:**
  - The verse from Proverbs, "Commit your plans to the Lord, and your thoughts will be established," (Proverbs 16:3, KJV) resonates perfectly with the idea of clarifying priorities with The Father. When we place our plans in His hands, it not only brings clarity but also grounds us in His purpose. This alignment with God's timing and will truly does make the journey more fulfilling and less overwhelming and we are more likely to HIT THE TARGET!

- o The *sabbatical* provided much-needed rest and realignment with divine purpose.
  - o The retreat facilitated significant personal reflection, spiritual growth, and professional development.
- **Receiving Divine Directives:**
  - o The Father wants to give us divine directives. We can receive clear directions and instructions on what we need to do or should be doing. If we never get still enough to hear, then we can spend a lifetime running in circles. My reflection is this, He's been orchestrating things in my life all this time and in yours as well. Again, it makes me think of David and how He knows that The Father "will instruct you and lead you in the way you should go," (Psalm 32:8). It is a beautiful reminder of His promise to guide us when we trust and listen.
- **Understand the assignment friend:**
  - o Understanding your assignment and the requirements for your season of productivity is crucial. Be sure that you understand all the requirements around what is mandated for your season. The directive to write and the subsequent discoveries have confirmed that I am on the right path (Hallelujah). These revelations through the Holy Spirit emphasizes the importance of everyone fulfilling their God-given roles and knowing who to connect with, whether it be to 'co-labor', support, or mentor and vice versa.

As we embrace our callings and walk in purpose, we should align ourselves with God's plans to include periods of "rest" as to effectively execute and contribute to the manifestation of His Kingdom on earth. So, I say to you:

- "Preach Preacher"
- "Prophesy Prophet"
- "Build and Send Apostles"
- "Evangelize Evangelists"
- "Teach Teachers"
- "Help Helpers"
- "Intercede Intercessors"
- "Worship Psalmists"
- "Write, Scribes Write!

I thank God for the special grace that has been released for us to accomplish great things for the Kingdom this season. Stay submitted and committed and be Spirit Led and Spirit Fed! Let's Excel in what He has established for us this season!

Appendices

Appendix A: Resources

Books, articles, and other references:

- https://www.merriam-webster.com/dictionary/mayhem
- https://www.merriam-webster.com/dictionary/sabbatical
- Holy Bible, King James Version (KJV).
- Psalm 32:8: "I will instruct thee and teach thee in the way which thou shalt go: I will guide thee with mine eye."
- Psalm 127:3-5: "Children are indeed a heritage from the LORD, and the fruit of the womb is His reward. Like arrows in the hand of a warrior, so are children born in one's youth. Blessed is the man whose quiver is full of them. He will not be put to shame when he confronts the enemies at the gate."
- Proverbs 16:3: "Commit thy works unto the LORD, and thy thoughts shall be established"
- Johnson, Theresa Harvard. Writing and The Prophetic: Foundations of The Scribal Anointing. Chamber of the Scribe, 2015.
- "Exploration of the role of the scribe and the scribal anointing, providing insights into the divine calling and purpose of writing as inspired by the Holy Spirit".

Personal Reflections and Experiences:

- Accounts of the 30-day sabbatical and the divine revelations experienced during this period. Memories and spiritual insights from childhood, as recalled during the sabbatical.
- Books, Courses, and Workshops on Writing and the Scribal Anointing.

- Materials and resources that were explored to understand "The role of the Scribe and the scribal anointing
- Discussions with Family Members, Conversations with my mother confirming early memories of reading, writing, and "playing school."
- Professional Training and Job Experiences through extensive training in communication, writing, and secretarial roles obtained through various job positions. Informal training through personal prayer time and learning to listen to God's voice and instructions.

www.ingramcontent.com/pod-product-compliance
Lightning Source LLC
Chambersburg PA
CBHW062105270326
41931CB00013B/3220